Bondages

Patrick Walton

Cadmus Publishing
www.cadmuspublishing.com

Copyright © 2023 Patrick Walton

Published by Cadmus Publishing
www.cadmuspublishing.com
Port Angeles, WA

ISBN: 978-1-63751-137-4

All rights reserved. Copyright under Berne Copyright Convention, Universal Copyright Convention, and Pan-American Copyright Convention. No part of this book may be reproduced, stored in a retrieval system, or transmitted in any form, or by any means, electronic, mechanical, photocopying, recording or otherwise, without prior permission of the author.

Table of Contents

Chapter 1 1
Chapter 2 7
Chapter 3 16
Chapter 4 30
Chapter 5 36
Chapter 6 42
Chapter 7 48
Chapter 8 60
Chapter 9 69
Chapter 10 76
About the Author 90

Chapter 1

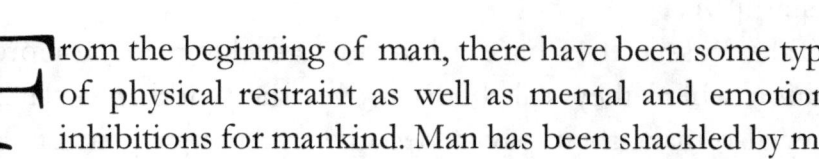

From the beginning of man, there have been some types of physical restraint as well as mental and emotional inhibitions for mankind. Man has been shackled by man or imprisoned to be able to control them. I would like to take you back to when the Egyptians enslaved the Hebrews. They were forced to slave for water and bread. They would separate the families and put them in bondages for their gain. There are so many forms of bondage in this world and always will be according to man. Now, man uses this tactic, which is the power to control, it gives him that superiority complex.

One seems to believe that they are better than you and they have the rights over you or the next person. According to my studies over the centuries, man has suffered from man's cruelty. There's always someone telling or forcing you to do things, or what you can and cannot do.

These are the ways of the world in which we live. Bondages became a way of life for most of civilization. A lot of different ethnic groups suffer worse than others all over the world. They were overseers like King David, King Solomon, who had servants that they ruled over, man and female. Physically they were their slaves, yet treated differently. There were those that lived and worked in the palaces that were treated differently than those that worked in the fields; those were beaten and forced to work without food or water. They all were in bondage. It was customary in that time frame according to history. As time moved forward, things changed, but not that much.

There is still a lot of bondage in the world we live in.

There's so much slavery still going on in the world today. People are being forced to do things they don't want to do just to stay alive.

Take Russia, they have a human trafficking ring for prostitution where they sell them all over the world into slavery. They also make them pay to become an American citizen, but they're not the only people like that; there's the Asians and Hispanics. They do it for a profit. They take the little girls and tell them, "If you want to ever see your family again, this is what you must do". Or if she has a child, they will kill her child if she doesn't do what they say. You see these things on TV so most of you think it's just a movie; yes, it's a show, but it's also what's happening in the world.

There are some wicked people in the world that prey on the weak; it's like they lack compassion for mankind. You know, it's kind of like the Pharaoh rule over the Hebrews, keeping them in bondage until they had rebuilt Egypt. They were treated so wrong and inhumane, but that was part of kinsmanship. Now that centuries have passed, the rulership is still there. It's only being done differently; there's still enslavement all over the world.

They kidnap people and sell or enslave them for their needs or demands, which I think is wrong, but who am I? Things like that go on in those third world countries like Kenya and Syria and that's the norm for those people. Then you have these different criminal organizations that traffic illegal people from their families. They force them to work in poppyfields to process heroin and cocaine, if you refuse, they kill you and ask who wants to be next.

Now, over in those third world countries, people fear for their life and safety from those that rule. As I read and studied, some of the things I came across amazed me. People are amazing, the way they do things. Especially the control they have. There's some cold-hearted people in the world; they have no compassion for human life. The only thing important to them is how they can control other people for their selfish gain or greed. I know that instructions are needed for man to live by, not to discredit anyone. I believe when you capture people against their will and then force them to do what you're scared to do and for the power, it's wrong. Because your reason for doing so is greed, gain, and the need to be in power. Looking at the big picture, it's about the haves and the have nots. Those that have prey on those that don't have and it goes around the world.

Where there's bondage, those that are under it are at a loss, they have no say in what happens. It's like living in the land of the lost and it's a heavy burden to carry. Take a country like Libya, that country suffers from bondage. It's a third world country with no government so those people live in fear for their safety everyday and they have no rights. Living in fear of your life or family members being taken away. The only law is the law of the land, meaning whatever tribe is the largest, that's who rules.

That's got to be a terrible way to live, under cruel and unjust punishment. This is what goes on around the world in which we live.

What a way for man to live--in fear. Why is man so wicked? Is it because of the control they get from forcing people to do the things they are afraid to do, or is it for power and the greed that comes from it?

There's so much corruption going on around the world, no matter where you are, it's there. Bondage is for real. People are living in fear. There's different cartels that enslave people for prostitution, manufacturing their drugs, and selling them off. These are the ways of the world. The people that do that call it trade.; it's part of the economy. It puts them on Wall Street.

It's human trafficking. It's wrong because no one should have the right to sell another person, but they do. Some of those cartels have a racket as to where a person can buy their citizenship to America. This is some of the corruption within the American government; they made it part of Wall Street. The things people will do for power and money. Now, God sent Moses to Egypt to deliver the Hebrews from bondages. What about the rest of the people in bondage? Where is their savior? How do they come from being under bondage, or do they? Who's there for them? Surely not you because you're under some form of bondage. That's about 63 to 68 percent of the people in the world.

They're selfish, only thinking about themselves and who they can use or step on to get some type of power. Ordinarily you would say that's crazy.

Face it. Look around you. What do you see? It's terrifying. It is so confusing to witness some of the events that mankind has to put up with in society, and there's really nothing you're able to do about the situation before you.

Everywhere in America there are different types of bondages. There are people in prison being mistreated by society; they suffer a rare form of bondage. They're told what, when, and how to do everything. They work for pennies on the dollar. They have been enslaved by the system. They call it modern slavery. They put you on a plantation and tell you what to do and if you refuse, they punish you.

I understand that prison was a choice for some, but where is the common respect for human life? It's bad enough you're away from your family as well as society. It's like the Willie Lynch letter, *The Making of a Slave.*

Where they separate the husband from his wife and children, and then separate the mother from her child in order to break them down and make them do what they needed them to do. Back in the 17th and 18th century here in this country, people of color were mostly enslaved and they were treated badly and wrongfully. They were also beaten and forced to slave for bread and water. The women were raped and sold off and they totally separated the families for control, and those they couldn't control were killed.

The Europeans went to different countries and stole ethnic groups of people and would take them back to Europe and enslave them. Once the Queen of England stated that there would not be slavery in Europe, they left Europe and immigrated Northwest to America to continue their slave trading. They sold them to former land owners. There was what's called "house negro" and "field negro". Now those that worked around the house were treated differently from those who worked in the fields. They were slaves from sun-up-till-sundown. That had to be a horrible way to live.

No matter how tired they were, if they stopped they were beaten. A lot of them tried to run away and every so often, one or two got away, but most of them were caught and beaten in front of the others and some were beaten to death. They were told, "This is what happens when you run." It's terrible to live in fear, but that's no way to have to live in fear of your safety. I hear a lot of people say it's hard times, but most of them don't even know what that means. When you have people being treated less than human, not knowing where their next meal is coming from or in fear of being molested. With no one to help you, for the fear of their own life. Now that's a hard way to have to live. Now, just imagine you were in that situation; how would you feel or deal with those issues you face day in and day out? Being fed like hogs, eating the waste, or not knowing if you're going to eat or not.

Take that country, Kenya, about 70 percent of that third world country suffers from AIDS and HIV. Those people have to drink the water they bathe in, as well as use the same water to cook with. I understand why they flee to America, so they can come from under the bondage they face.

There is so much sadness in the world we live in. Now, I want to share a little history with you about this country. This land belonged to Native Americans (or Indians, now). Those Europeans came to this country, and after they try to tell you that Christopher Columbus discovered this country. How are you going to discover something that's already there? People were already here, it's not like there weren't any lifeforms here when they landed.

Chapter 2

So, here's what the Europeans did; they came over and stole all of the land that they could and they raped the women and killed them off. Then the rest of them were gathered up and they put them on what they call a reservation. The white men made those people all kinds of promises to them and in the process, they killed thousands of those Indians. And that was alright for them to do in order to gain control of this country. This has been going on for centuries all over the world.

Ever since there have been people, there has been some form of bondage. It's like you do as I say, not as I do, or suffer the punishment. It's all about control and with control comes power and power brings fear. You have all these oppressed people all over the world that're in a confused state of mind, scared to talk or act and not knowing what to do. It's like they're faced with a lose/lose situation with no help. Living in bondage, you really don't have any rights.

The overseers are in control and they are able to do as they will with you and your kind. Your freedom is lost; you're trapped in a cage like an animal. Society is alright with people living in bondage, it's the only way they are in control. Especially when it benefits them. For some people it's a trade, people are a trade good to buy and sell all over the world. People don't like to talk about things like bondage or forcing others to do things against their will. See, they make movies about different things and, for the most part, people would assume it's for entertainment, right? True, but it's also telling you about what's happening in society. That's like Donald Trump being the President of America; before it happened, people said it never would happen, but then it did. Hm, imagine that, unbelievable.

When a person, or people, have any type of authority to dictate what someone can or cannot do or where they can go. Now, for those that refuse or become rebellious there's a great punishment for them. Depending on the situation or circumstances, death could be the punishment.

For a person to have that much authority or power to say who lives or who dies is very overwhelming. When you become someone's property, you must do as they say or suffer the consequences for not doing as you were told.

Take King David, he once killed a man because he didn't like the way he was treating his wife. Because he was king, he was able to do so. There's people like him all over the world; the world is trapped in bondages of some kind. That will never change. So, don't think it will.

That's only from my point of view; when you have dictators here in this country, they're in charge. It's like you are damned if you do, damned if you don't. God only knows what's next. It's strange now because if you don't do what they say, there are consequences for your actions. Bondage is real and it will always exist in the world in which you live.

Back to television, the information box that tells you what's going on around the world. A lot of people say "Oh, that's bull", but it's one and the same; it's entertainment, but it's also real. Look at it like looking through a telescope at the stars, is that real? Like having people enslaved is real, it does exist, and there's nothing you can do about it.

It's all part of what goes on in the world. Some people call it racism. Those of royalty prey on the underclass people.

My grandfather was the first and only black man I witnessed say "mister" to. Now, for him to say "Mr. Charlie" to Poppa, he had to be of some type of importance to them. I'm from Mississippi and during that time they still had plantations and the color/black people at that time were called "boy", "buck", or "negro", and a lot of families lived on that plantation and they farmed the land. Most of them weren't paid money and the one who was the landowner had a dry good store for them to shop at. Whatever money they made they spent it back with the landowner. That was called sharecropping.

I wish I had been a part of my daughter's life. That way I would have been able to take her there just for her to be able to know something about a different lifestyle. Outside of that suffering and abuse. You would have to be able to see what some of those Southern people had to live with. Having no running water in the house or pumping water from the well. By the grace of God, some of them made it.

There are so many different cultures in the world. Now, to be taken away from that to something new. That person would have some sense of fear, not knowing where they are or what to do. I'm sure at that point, your survival skills come into play because you're afraid, confused, and unsure of your safety. This is where you become physically, mentally, and emotionally. It causes your mentality to change and you're an emotional wreck due to the situation you're faced with. That's a hell of a situation for a person to deal with every day of their life.

Sure there's different reasons why people feel like you're their property and that they can do whatever they want. Now, no one knows why those people feel like that; is it because of the power to control? I mean, no one knows man's intentions or motives for doing things like that to others. Because you're not their property.

No matter where you are or what you're doing, there are rules and policies you just follow, that's where law and order come in at. Man must have rules to live by. That doesn't make it right to enslave people for their gain or greed. There's nothing right about slavery, but it's allowed all over the world. People are still being forced to do things against their will as of today. Our society uses hidden racism. They try to hide it, but are unable to do so; it's a known fact that those of wealth or collateral stick together to maintain control. It's like the game of chess.

Protect those most important possessions, whether it be land, people, oil, drugs, or even money. By doing so, there's some type of bondage behind their actions. They need to continue slave labor and trade.

Without that, they're no better off than you. It's been going on for so long that it's the norm in our society. It's like no one cares about life or what goes on around them, which is sad. Now, how would you react after seeing your mother, daughter, or sister being raped and beaten and you or no one else was there to stop it?

That's only some of the torture that goes on that's not talked about; society doesn't want to deal with that issue because interferes with those in control.

After all has come to pass that man is king and ruler of the land and everything on it, but, that being said, the soul of that man is doomed and his emotional state is damaged. Plus, he's a mental wreck. For all that don't believe that, there's a force greater than thee. Ask yourself, "What keeps me going?" Even in the sense of bondage. God has a purpose for everything and everyone under the sun. So, along the way be mindful of your actions towards others because we're all in some form of bondage.

I would like you to take a look at society and ask yourself, "What's got me trapped?" Then, and only then, will you begin to understand enslavement. It's different for everyone, but it's still bondage.

Bondage is real and for most it's the same from a mental, emotional, and psychological view. It's the breakdown that causes the most damage. It causes suicide, as well as harm to others.

Here's what happens; they put you on these different psychic changes to alter your mind even more and tell you, "You're depressed and this medicine here is good for that." That's one more lost to society, which is another form of control. Now, I'm able to stick you in a mental hospital and claim you unfit for society. These are just some of the challenges you face in our society. There's some cruel and selfish people in the world we live in. This pain seems so unreal for man to be able to handle, yet he does it well. Everyone has their own point of view about. One thing is for sure and two for certain, at the end of the day the bondage is the same. The torture and punishment of the enslaved people of the world.

I want to talk a little bit about being in an emotional state of bondage. When you become emotionally drained from being mistreated, misused, or even punished over and over, and then being made to do things against your will. It starts to break you down mentally. I believe that no man should have that right to treat anyone that way, but in order to be in control they use it as a mental bondage. Living in fear can be dangerous; it's like living in servitude and some don't want to live enslaved and life for them has no value so they give it up.

Everyone has a breaking point and once you get to that point, your emotions are wrecked, you lose focus, and give up on life. Emotionally, everyone suffers from being told or forced to do something and when they can do it. That's how this system we live by was designed for man. There is no way around it and it's been going on since the beginning of man. People have been forced to do things since Adam and Eve.

To break a person's spirit gives you the power over them. You become the master and they become the slave. That's power. I, myself, believe that it is wrong to force anyone to do things against their will. Now that's just me and others might view it differently due to their circumstances. I mean, I'm alright with laws and rules, as it gives some form of guideline for man to abide by. To mistreat people for your own personal gain or greed is wrong. All through the Bible, it talks about some form of slavery and how they were treating people.

They emotionally broke them down and physically forced them to work for nothing. They barely fed them and they also took everything they had. Even now, it's still going on all over the world.

At some point, a person becomes uncertain, which leads to them becoming emotionally unbalanced and that causes a mental breakdown. Ask yourself, "Why me? Am I not worth it or am I worthless, is life worth living?"

These are some of the questions a person asks themself. Everyone has their own theory about the things that happen around them. I believe you would have to observe the facts in order to be able to understand or accept what's happening at that moment. Being emotionally damaged has got to be rough. I couldn't even begin to imagine how or what it would be like to be in that situation. Sure, I'm in some form of bondage, but not as a servant to others. I'm kind of sympathetic when it comes to misusing or mistreating people as it's inhumane. Where's the humanity in that?

Everyone has misfortune in life; you don't have to prey on the weak. There's so many who do that. The people that have to live under that strain or stress, it's sad, but it's the way of the world that we live in.

Now, there's some that like being beaten, whipped, and even forced to do things. If they're not being treated that way. They don't feel loved or wanted. Some of you would say that's crazy; it is, but it's true.

Emotionally, their state of being is wrecked, which transfers to their mental state being damaged. It's crazy, but there's something about pain that drives people. In one sense, I don't understand, but in another sense, I do because it's what they're used to and know. Now, I will agree it's strange but it's real.

Take those sadists, they endure pain and it's like they get gratification from inflicting pain and torture to themselves and others. Mentally and physically. It's like they're heartless with no compassion for the next person. Those people are willing to sacrifice their life and others for control or entertainment.

Now, there are three stages of slavery: physical, emotional, and mental. Earlier, I spoke briefly about them. Now, I want to try and explain the difference between them. Most of you would say slavery is slavery right to some degree. Physically is when you inflict pain or torture in order to control them or get them to do whatever you wanted them to do.

Emotionally: deals with your feelings; it makes a person emotive, which dominates how you feel or act towards an event which happened to that person. It is an intense feeling surrounded by fear. People that suffer from that despair. It's like an inhabited arousement that has something to do with your self-worth. I would like to put emphasis on this situation as it also affects your mood; some people do that behavior for attention with no regard for the other person. Now, take that woman, the prostitute, she likes being dominated and discriminated against by her trick or manager, who takes her money and treats her like she's nothing and has no respect for her.

Mentally: a person becomes irrational to reality and the only thing that matters is to do what their master says. It's like a drug; you use it and it becomes the most important thing in your life. That person becomes deranged and their mind develops a mental deficiency which affects their thoughts and behavioral patterns. Now, people have what's called a core belief system that starts at a child level. This affects how and what that child believes in from how they were raised up. Let's say all you did was beat your child and once that child grows up, their belief system is if they're not beaten then they're not loved. If I tell you, "Your daddy ain't shit," what effect does that have on that child? If that child is taught negativity, then their belief system tells them they're worthless or they have to beat or be beaten to express love. It makes it hard for them to make a social adjustment with society.

Some of them have a very low I.Q. percentage and they also suffer from some form of depression which comes from a mental disorder of the mind. Most of them carry around a poor belief system and they feel like you don't understand them. And they're right because you won't take the time to listen to what's going on with them. Cognitively, you can help them rebuild a new belief system with self talk. Using I statements that will begin a road to success.

Chapter 3

Only you can break the bondages you face. Not to say it's going to be easy, but you can and will be successful because you are important, as well as worthy. Now, before I continue to stress the bad about bondage, there's some good that comes from being in bondage.

You have some freedom: you can work and be paid for your work, you're able to buy a home, car, and other things of that nature. There's also laws and rules put into effect to live by, so you won't be a savage or uncultivated or without civilization. I have dealt with people of all walks of life. I've learned that they all have something in common.

The need to express their views. Sometimes all it takes is for someone to say that they understand. Everyone has their own dealing in life. Some were good, some were bad, but, at the end of the day, you're still here, so you have a chance to change your situation.

By making better decisions, selecting different types of people to be around, and by doing different things, you'll begin to feel a difference in your life because if you always do what you've always done, you're always going to get what you've always gotten. At some point, a person gets tired of losing. Now, if you want something different, you have to do something different.

Because anything you're involved with starts with you. You're in control of your situation, not me. Things may be complex or even complicated. In some cases the situation may not be voluntary. A person can and will be forced against their will and that's the part of bondage I'm talking about, where greed comes in and causes harm to others for one's personal reasons.

By thinking outside the box using cognitive thinking processes, you are able to develop different views; positively, you begin to have and build better relationships with others. You'll slowly come from under some of that bondage of the oppressor. For centuries, people have been oppressed and enslaved. To be crushed by the abuse of authority.

That gives one control over another is a burden,it saddens the heart of those you love and that love you. It also brings about a form of depression. Because it affects you mentally and spiritually, it's a hardship that's so severe one could only imagine the suffering that a person goes through from being physically, emotionally, mentally, and spiritually broken. Throughout life you're going to have to do things you don't want to do in order to be able to do something you want or need to do in order to survive. About one out of five make it through the enslavement that is forced on them.

Now, ask yourself, "Is this part of God's plan for man and, if so, why must it continue to exist? Haven't there been enough executions over the centuries of bondage? Why is there so much destruction in the world which we live in, despite the turmoil and the suffering that goes on?"

A person gets to the point where they are physically broken, emotionally damaged, and mentally wrecked and there's nothing left to do to that person.

Let's say the percent of survivors are about 7 out of 10 that actually survive the severe punishment from the oppressor.

There comes a time when man should ask himself what if the situation was different, where he was being enslaved or oppressed, how would he feel about the bondage he faces.

The Bible states that there's a time and place for everything under the Sun. Now does that mean I will become king and be able to rule over others or will I have servants? You know there are some things that are changeable and those things you can change, but there are also things that are unchangeable and bondage is one of them.

Throughout life, you'll face many different challenges that you will have to deal with and some challenges are unjust. You have to be able to accept it and move forward. It's kind of like being disable; there's nothing you can do about that, it's one of life's situations you face.

In the physical state you're at a loss, but mentally, your mind is free from illness. Everyone has their own issues. It's amazing how people are able to endure the enslavement and torture and maintain their dignity because it's so easy to give up or be manipulated by the influence of others. We live in a society where the rich prey on the poor. Your oppressor knows that you're in a helpless state, so he applies more pressure to keep you in that state of being.

I am prejudiced when it comes to enslavement or people because it's an unpleasant act on the less fortunate class of people. Mainly the people of color and they have fortitude to overcome whatever the oppressor puts before them. I'm sure that distress plays a part in their discomfort, yet they endure. It's very disgusting, knowing there's nothing you can do about being enslaved.

I discovered that, for some people, that the only life they know is to be forced to do, but that doesn't make it right. Some would say they only have the power that you give them, but that's not true. Yes, they do have the power to control what you do, to a degree, by being in captivity.

You're corralled up like cattle being held against your will and forced to slave for nothing. Now the captor is the overseer. Now you realize you're at a loss. Take those people that are incarcerated; they are told when to sleep, work, and even when they can shower. That is just how serious this bondage system is. It's like you're worthless; the only good you serve is to be a slave. They say you have rights. What rights do you have? You don't own your home, car, or even the money you make. Because, just like they let you get it, they can take it. This is the society we live in.

In America, prison is a big business; it's on Wall Street and you have to be wealthy to buy stock. It's a big plantation that warehouse people to work for pennies and the taxpayers are forced to support it. They warehouse you for a profit, sure, I get when people commit a crime and get caught there is a punishment for that crime. Once they lock you up, the court did not sentence you to labor. You become even more enslaved, you're being mistreated, and there is no fairness. You're no longer part of society. So see, there's really no freedom in this world we live in.

The world is so mixed-up and selfish until you're either the predator or the prey. The oppressor is always forcing the oppressed. It's been that way and it will always be that way; it's one of the unchangeable things. It's the world and you know where you fit in.

It's almost like a no win situation, the only one who wins are those in charge. Even the working people are in bondages because they have to pay taxes on things that are not theirs; then you're being told what and when you can or can not do. Now, you can be naive and think it doesn't apply to you, but, if you're not from the wealthy upper class part of society, then it fits. There's rulers all over the world and they get together and discuss their needs and wants. Now, if they want to do an experiment they pick a country in a small place and test whatever it is they want exposed to the world, but, first, they have to know how it works or if it works.

You have all these scientists all over the world experimenting with different chemicals that they use on people for reactions. They do this as a form of control. They call it science and we're the subjects. I want to expound further about how corrupt this system is; those people segregate people into groups and pick what you do and where you do it. Wall Street is this country because they buy and sell 24 hours a day, and those people in prison are state employees, but not making state wages. It's called modern day slavery under the 14th Amendment, it is how they get away with it.

Now, everyone has their own views about different situations but, it's a racket, it's all part of their politics, they make it suitable for them and their kind.

Most third world countries do not have a government to govern the people, so whoever has the most valuables or people rule that region.

They dictate the law of the land. It gives them the power to enslave people for their gain.

Then their drug addiction is another form of bondage because that person or people have become dependent on that substance, whether it is alcohol or drugs, eventually it takes control of that person. Depending on the substance, that person is not able to function without it. It alters their ability to perform different tasks and it affects their mood.

Because it is a mind altering drug and it is part of that cycle of boindage society faces. When the wicket comes contempt comes also, so he who preys on the weak shall harvest destruction for they know their wrongs. By doing so, they punish you for their wrongs. They endanger you and your kind for the sake of enslavement.

It would be insane for a person to think they're free. Because, no matter where you are or what you do, there's someone to dictate what you do or have. There's no way around it. It's been that way and always will be that way.

Life is like a football game, there's rules applied. You have the owners, the general managers, coach, assistant coach, offense trainer, defense trainer, and the team; everyone is told what to do. In order to be part of an organization, you must abide by the conditions. Now, that's what our society consists of.

The world in which we live is so organized, the administrative structure that was set in place for you to follow took a whole lot of planning to where you as a people, have to be marshall. They designed a system for people to obey or suffer the consequences for not doing so. They call it law. This is why the different organizations from all over the world are in control of the world. Some would say the president, governor, congress, state representatives, or the student body. Here's what they did, they had an idea about how to rule a region. They laid out the foundation and this group of people got together and took over the area and controlled everything there. So they all agreed to follow the plan and lives were lost from both parties, but they were willing to sacrifice to become successful. Now, that is what it takes to be successful; be willing to do whatever it takes to accomplish your goal.

When it comes to bondage, it is essential for laws and rules to be put in place. Otherwise there wouldn't be any type of structure in the world.

As you now know, there are some things that will never be changed and bondage is one of them. Even the Bible talks about tithes and taxes. You're supposed to give the land owner his taxes and give God his tithes. So being under laws and rules is nothing new.

Living in today's society, you're either part of the problem or part of the solution. Now if you're part of the problem or causing the problem, meaning you're interfering with the development, that is not allowed. Now you're creating another problem and they don't like that. So, you or your party must be subtracted from society. Because if a lot of people start to think and act like you, that resistance comes into play. Those in power become uneased because you're starting a system of rebelliousness and our society will not tolerate that from society as a whole.

Now, you're trying to break the chain of command, and that interferes with the bondage foundation. Now, when and if those different councils become aware or threatened by your action. They will find ways to eliminate the said parties that pose a threat. There are consequences for your actions. In the world we live, you are damned if you do, damned if you don't. For the most part, it's their world and we're just in it, we are what's called collateral goods.

From a political viewpoint, their concerns are about policies that determine what's happening now and the future looks like that's the course of action they take, they have a plan.

This group of people get together and discuss and talk about what action they want to take next. To make sure everyone is together on the project.

Like the government they got together with the rulers of the world and created the COVID-19 virus to kill off people all over the world. They knew it would create some kind of despair for the people. You think they cared. Probably not; you must remember we're collateral damage. They needed to destroy some of the world population without just outright killing them off. The system they live by there's no room for overcrowding the population.

It had gotten to the point where they no longer knew how many people were in the world and it was becoming uncontrollable. So those leaders from around the world got together and agreed to this plot and put it in effect without the lower class of society knowing until it happened. They discussed this in 2005 and had it in plan for 2018, but in 2010 there was talk about a vaccine for it.

It wasn't until 2021 when they developed the cure for it, now, they hid it for as long as they could.

The government was so hesitant to expose it to the people once they did. They used all kinds of trickery, deception, and schemes for society to believe they were working on a cure for the disease they created.

It only shows the people who and what they're dealing with, now, look at how many families lost their homes, jobs, and loved ones due to this virus.

Do you think the government cares about your loss? Now, the money that they are giving the U.S. citizens or, should I say, the taxpayers. They're going to have to pay that back. They say the government is for the people, but what people? The wealthy, because they're sure not for the poor. It was designed for the purpose of control.

In doing my research, I discovered that the American people are alright with the way things are. Only because they believe there's nothing they can do about the situation they face. Which is true because they're the minority. In society all over the world people think the same way. Why? Because there has always been a dictator since there have been people and there always will be.

Now, some of you might have uncertainty or inclination not to believe or accept the truth and you have that God-given right to do so.

I'm not exposing the system for you to become dismayed or discouraged from these texts, this is only my point of view about society.

As you go through life you learn different things and everyone has their own paths, each one has something to do on their journey. We all learn different trades as you go through life. Be mindful of your actions and remember, you're no better or worse than the next person. Everyone has faults and we all suffer from some sort of bondage in some form or another. So don't be judgemental when it comes to people because you're human and it would be inhumane to judge others.

You know, there are some good benefits from being in bondage, you're able to have things like cars, homes, and all of the basic things in life; you're not totally a slave with no freedom, it just has its limits. Everyone is not being forced to labor for nothing like the 1700s where people were in slavery by force, meaning work or die.

I always hear people talk about beating the system and knowing nothing about the system they want to beat. Now, back when there were slave states and the plantation owners owned you, he did whatever he wanted to do as far as raping the women to taking the children and selling them off to killing the men, and whatever else came to mind.

Now, as far as beating the system, first and foremost, you cannot beat something you don't know anything about, so in order to bear the system, you must first learn the part of the system you want to beat, meaning you must become part of the system. For instance, take the vaccine made for the COVID-19 virus. It was developed for the American people, but the last to get it. The American government really doesn't care about you. Because, if they did, they would make sure the country is alright first. America is the trade center of the world.

They were more worried about those other countries and what they could do for them, with no concern for the American people. Did you know that the American currency can be used all over the world, but you can't use any other country's currency except Canada's here in this country. That should say a lot about America.

This country suffers from homelessness, sickness, crime, and also our civilization is under attack by this virus that was created by the government and they want to blame another country for the disaster they made across the world. No one wants to talk about that. Why? Because it hits home. God forbid you for exposing the government for their lack of duty to the American citizens.

Now that the epidemic has hit this country like a hurricane, that's the least of their worries. It left a lot of the lower class American people unemployed, homeless, and the government doesn't really want to help the American people that are taxpayers out of this crisis they are facing. The American people are okay with it because they feel there's nothing they can do about the situation they are currently facing.

You are all protesting about Black Lives Matter. Well, what about All Lives Matter? You all work and pay all these different taxes for times like this and they aren't there for the working class people. You all put these politicians in offices to govern the affairs of the American people and they do nothing. Aren't they supposed to represent you as a people or at least that's what they said to get you to vote.

Where the leadership for the people of America. It's not about the little man, it's all about the wealthy that group and stick together when they're wrong, but say they're right. In order to continue to keep you in bondage.

Now, they still have physical bondage, but mostly it's emotional and mental bondage, because if they can keep you in a confused or depressed state of being they can control. Then you become stressed out. Being pressured into a form of depression, then they put you on antidepressants. Then some turn to street drugs. Like heroin and cocaine or crystal meth to hide their emotional and mental state of being. This is how our government deals with lower class society. With drugs and alcohol, one of the pacifiers they use for control.

Where is your savior when you need him because in Egypt when the Pharaoh ruled, the Hebrew savior was Moses, he delivered them out of bondage. Maybe some of you will realize what's happening to us as a people; you're just a tool for them to use as needed, you're worth nothing.

America is this big plantation with many shareholders and you're not one of them, you're one of the slaves. Meaning you do as they say, not as they do.

The tax money they take from you they use for other countries. They destroy that country so they can rebuild it, stick a flag, and then you're one of our allies, only because it's something they want from that country. Now they do nothing for the American citizens but walk over them. Now, talking about the people who voted for you to oversee the country and the States in this country, you believe them when they said they would make things better. Are things better for the American people? Probably not. From the history of the world to the present day, much hasn't changed except there's more mental abuse today than ever.

This country is at an unrest state at this time with all this racial discriumination where the white police are killing unarmed black people. Then there are those people with that superior attitude where they think they're inferior to others. You know there's still that physical abuse caused by them killing people of color. You can say it's not like that and that would only mean you're on their team. Because if you think you're not in bondage because you have a home, bank account, and a car. Which are the basics in today's society.

Hate to be the one to tell you that at any moment, they can take it all away. There's nothing you can do about it. At the end of the day, you're a slave and you have got to work on their farm. You're still under their control.

Some of you might say, "What do you mean?" Let's just say you were told not to drive and you got caught driving. Now if they kill you it would be okay because you broke the law and that's the punishment they saw fit for you.

Who's to say they can't do that? Remember who's in control. It's the law and rules they made for people like us, the lower class bracket.

There's not much of a difference from being able to move freely as to being confined. We all suffer from being under their control; some suffer more severe control than others. Yes, you do have the right to choose what you want and don't want to do and don't do, but there's consequences for your negative actions. The hidden reality is you have no authority. Ask yourself, "Am I the puppet or the puppet master?" For the most part, you're the puppet due to your status. The lower class bracket really doesn't have a say on what happens in society as a whole. I don't know if any of you are familiar with the six degrees of separation. Here's the steps that need to be taken: first, you don't know the mayor who knows the senator, who knows the State Attorney General, who knows the Governor, who knows someone in Congress who can get to the U.S. Attorney General who then goes to the President, and there's no guarantee you will be heard then.

Now, as far as those people below the poverty level, they're at a total loss. Because a lot of them are unemployed, homeless, or drug addicted and they don't pay taxes. Not talking about any specific ethnic group. When dealing with the system, you must view all parts. That way, you know how to address a certain situation. You have to figure out what you want to do and then figure out where you fit in. If you don't fit in, then figure out what you need to do to get there. It's a process and it can be done; the question is, what are you willing to do to get there? These are some of the tools for success. Only you can determine your future. Some people live in a delusional world because they don't want to face reality. They don't want to take responsibility for themselves. A lot of people want something for nothing. Then you have some fear exposed and don't want to face life's challenges. At some point, a person needs to be able to step out of their comfort zone in order to progress in life of achievement. Which requires action, which is gained by effort. You need these skills: determination, dedication, and discipline, which are the three things you need to acquire success.

That being said, there's thirteen principles to life.

Chapter 4

Those principles are stated 1) you must have love for the next person as God has love for you. 2) Truth-you should be truthful to yourself and others. 3) Peace-keep a peaceful spirit. 4) Freedom-to have a free spirit, if either of those first four are violated then justice must be served. 6) Loyalty-you must stand firm for what you believe in. 7) Life-so as you live, you should want others to live and help along the way. 8) Love is something everyone needs. 9) Death-it's the only thing you can't escape; just as you're willing to live for what you believe in, you should also be willing to die for it as well. 10) Dishonor-so as you live for the cause, also be willing to die as well because if it isn't worth fighting for then it isn't worth having. 11) You will seek knowledge. 12) You will get an understanding. 13) Wisdom will set in as you go along.

Now, for those that are willing to live by these principles, your future is bright. Keep your faith and continue to do what's good, it will make this bondage easier for some. People want something but don't want to do what it takes to accomplish what they want. It's an old saying, if it isn't worth working for then it isn't worth having. There's some truth in that. Keep in mind, for the most part you are in total control of your actions. There is a guideline for people to live by, according to man. Yes, there must be some kind of structure for man to follow, otherwise the human race would live like savages or barbarians with really no regards to civilization and no culture. That's why law and order are needed for society. It's one of the most important things needed in civilization. That's a good thing because it determines the present and helps make future decisions for a better society.

Everyone has their own view or perception about things. Now, there's what's called socialism, they're one of those elite groups of people, they're something like capitalism, the only difference is socialism deals with the political movement; it's the Marxists that set the stage for capitalism, it's the economic system that's put in place to invest capital for a profit, this principle is used to enslave people so they can benefit from them. Which means they have the authority over who does what, where, and how it's to be done. It also brings about social interaction where we are able to live and breed and form some type of relation. Which brings us back to control.

Furthermore, in understanding bondage, there's some need for it, without it there would be no leadership in the world and it would be in a state of confusion. Look at where we are today compared to centuries ago. Our civilization has improved, we're more together now than ever. We still have success in progress. There's still some cruel people in the world.

Their selfishness won't allow them to advance with time. It's so inhumane the way people are treated. So I guess there is no way around that, even in bondage we are still able to advance and move forward.

There are crises we have to face, we just have to stay focused on the future. You know the past, that's not what we want as a people.

Now, man is so creative and intelligent that they have designed an electronic automobile, these are things society can use as we move forward. This is some of what coming together for a greater cause can do. Like I stated earlier, being part of a team and working together is what our government should be focusing on.

This country was built on leadership. I would like to believe that one of the reasons for a government is for the people of this country. Yes, about 75% of this country are foreigners; this is the history of America. So you would think the reason for politicians is for the people, right? Now, let's not get it wrong, all of them aren't greedy or selfish. As people, some of you become egotistic, you feel you're better than those that are not wealthy or well off. Which makes it hard for others to deal with you. I believe everyone is important and no one should be misused or abused for someone else's gain. So, when dealing with people, be mindful of the next person because we all need each other to progress in life. It will ease some of the burden we suffer from this bondage we're under as a whole. It's a work in progress, as we move forward the chains are loosening up and there's not as much tension as there once was. Keep in mind, it's not all about you.

Remember, whatever you're dealing with, there's zillions dealing with something worse than others. We're all human so why not show love instead of hate? By knowing the odds are against you, when we as a people put our pride aside and form a union and work towards a solution to the problems we face day in and day out. Because if we don't do it, then who will?

If you think about it, you are your brother's keeper. Even in bondage, there's compassion, it's not all sorrow, shame, fear, or hurt. It's a way of life.

I was reading a scripture and it said, "He who has a deceitful heart finds no good. And He who has a perverse tongue falls into evil."

That scripture defines some of those politicians that you elect to govern over you. With all their tricks and lies and fake promises they make to get elected. I know. You're probably saying you have to pick someone. Yes, it's a chance to believe them or it sounded good you voted for them to fill a position.

Now ask yourself, "If I was elected governor of a state, what would I do? Would I do something for myself or for the people of the state to make things better for the working class people?" Something like raising sales taxes or lowering property taxes, lowering property rental so people could afford to rent and have somewhere to live. Build housing for the homeless. These are some of the issues statewide that no one wants to discuss because then you're talking about helping society. Those in power don't want that because it interferes with the power.

Those are only a few of the issues that are not talked about or exposed. Keep in mind, it's all about the decisions that determine the outcome. Whatever project you do set in motion. Everyone has their own opinion or view about things. Now, what role do you take in society that can benefit society as a whole? It's awful that most of you don't want to see a person be successful and are willing to do whatever it takes to prevent their success.

Most people are caught up in that selfish cycle. Well, I want to expose this theory to you all. We are all users, it's the only way for anything to progress. I use you and you use them; in essence, we all need each other for things to get done. Now dealing with the political views of bondage, it's an overall subject. Society likes to blame the politicians for the crooks in the streets, not enough street lights, things like that. On the other hand, politicians blame society and make things harder for them to buy using things like needing more funding to do roadwork or needing funding for school teachers. It's all a racket where the rich get richer and the poor get poorer.

It's a give and take situation. Everybody wants to win and nobody wants to lose. You're going to have winners as well as losers. There's a part of life where a person should make sure they're together and secure. You need to understand. Because how are you going to help someone else when you're messed up? So, I would like to think it would be safe to say that nobody is going to treat you like you treat yourself--your good, bad, and indifference.

As I've been explaining my views about bondage, I expect some of you probably assume or consider to be obligated to my views as an introduction of reality and that's okay. This is just one of the topics I engage in. Things that deal with life and what part man has to do with it. I discovered that man has everything to do with society as a whole. You know they say knowledge is the key. Now, that being said, the government has all these different secret locations where they study and do all kinds of testing. They created the coronavirus for the sole purpose to kill off people all over the world for population control. It's disgusting to think how cruel man can be; they try to be discreet and hide it from society.

Gradually it's coming out and people are beginning to witness the truth and they can no longer hide it. The United States government is creating these different diseases and blaming other countries. Not to say that they don't have the science and technology to do so, but it's that the U.S. knows what's going on around the world.

You know there's a lot of people of power and influence that have a say on what's going on in the world.

Chapter 5

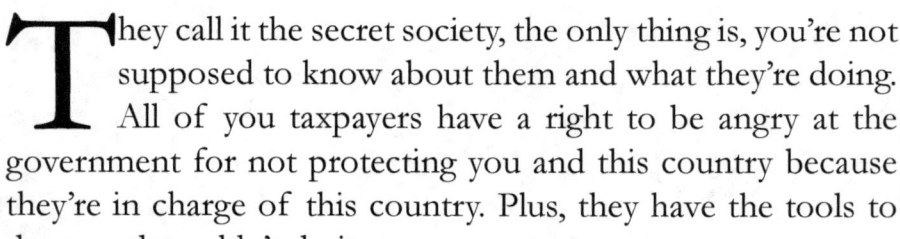

They call it the secret society, the only thing is, you're not supposed to know about them and what they're doing. All of you taxpayers have a right to be angry at the government for not protecting you and this country because they're in charge of this country. Plus, they have the tools to do so and wouldn't do it.

As you all are aware of the propaganda that's going on in America at the present time caused by those in charge. A lot of society says he's done some good things for America. Like the economic system, economically there were some improvements in jobs and trades, but it wasn't for the lower class citizens.

In some states, people are unable to afford to rent a place to live for being overpriced. That only drives the homeless population up. Take states like Illinois, Minnesota, Colorado, and a few others. This country has more people than jobs. That is another reason for the pandemic that they exposed the world to.

The government ignores its responsibility to the people of the United States and would rather focus on other country's problems. The leader of this country is more concerned with Iran, Iraq, and North Korea and about what they're doing over there when the home front is in dangerous times. There's so much wrong in this country; people being forced out of their homes, loss of employment, kids out of school, I'm talking about the taxpayers. Those are the people that pay these taxes for security on their property and safety. The crime rate is up due to lack of employment for the citizens. This epidemic that was created got out of control because they were unable to account for all of the people in the world. They were losing control. They panicked!

Throughout the generations there has been adversity among the people. I've seen the hurt in people's faces, some spirits broken. Yet, they keep faith and look for change. What good is it to be wealthy with no soul?

There is an evil which I have seen under the sun, it seems to be common among man. Why is that? I don't know, is it for capitalism, socialism, or communism. It could be all of the above; they're one in the same. Then it may just be some greedy and evil soul. I'm almost sure there are and always will be. This world isn't all bad, there's good as well, but people don't look at the good, only the bad. Because they need someone or something to blame. We live in a society that likes to point fingers and say, "I told you so." That doesn't solve problems. Where's the ownership, who's taking the responsibility for that act? There's another form of bondage I mentioned earlier, it's about prison, it's a physical state of being, as well as a mental state. Now, some of society seem to believe that locking you up, away from society, family, and friends is a form of physical punishment. Then you have those that imprison themselves mentally with drugs, alcohol, and antidepressants; it's all a form of control. People do things for different reasons and only they know the reason. Those that commit a crime and are sent to prison as a penalty for a length of time. While there, you're being told what, where, when, and how to do or act; there's prison rules also that you follow and if you don't, you'll be punished for that, too. Here in America, it has changed so they don't beat you anymore, now they put you in segregation for a while and take a good time from you for disobeying their laws and rules. Then you have drug addicts and alcoholics who intoxicate themselves to avoid life. Something happened in their life that pushed them to drugs or alcohol that they use as a crutch so they don't have to deal with their problems. Either way, it's sad that the society we live in has caused that much pain to people as a whole.

Because that form of bondage is a very scary situation, it's a vicious cycle as that addiction progresses, it becomes more dangerous. At that point, all that person wants is that substance and some depending on the substance at whatever cost.

It can, and will, drive a person insane and others to kill for it. It's not that person, it's the substance that has the control.

Man suffers from the weakness of the things of the world, which also puts him in bondages like greed, lust, envy, and jealousy; these are some of man's downfalls, because he will kill or die for those reasons. Greed is full of selfishness, it's all about that individual. Take our last president, he's Pharoah, he wants to rule the world. First, he's not a politician so his knowledge about politics is little. He is a corrupt businessman. Now, as for those that rule the world, they didn't want a female to be president of this country and they used him as their scapegoat until he felt he was in charge. He was to the point where his soldiers raided Capitol Hill because he felt the election was stolen from him and didn't want to be replaced with a new Pharoah. Ever since, I have been able to understand the Republicans and the Democrats are one in the same, the spokesman for the people. So, no matter who the commander-in-chief is, they're in it together. It's them against us, you can say. They're wealthy and you're poor.

That's where sacrifice comes into play. What are you willing to do to be in charge? Everyone has a limit, what's yours?

There is a parable that goes like this, "Concerning the sons of man, God test them, that they may see themselves as animals."

We are living in a time that has already passed. Now, President Trump thinks he's lord and ruler of this country, it's his way or no way.

That's why the American people are scared to act against him and his Republicans for their wrongs. Some of them that helped make him lord and ruler want to strip his powers away. No matter who's lord and ruler there will still be bondage. There's no way around it. The best thing is to keep faith and don't give up, the worst is yet to come for the son of man.

Always remember you're not alone, so get up because united we stand and divided we fall; it seems like you're down, but not out, take a stand and become a part of society. It's a saying, faith without work is a dead deed.

Whatever is happening in this country is happening somewhere else; this is not the only country suffering from the oppressor of man. This too shall pass, then man will continue to prey on mankind because that's the cycle in which we live by. He's never pleased!

Through time, there have been some types of conflict with man and there always will be. They say there's a time and place for everything under the sun.

So, imagine it's time as a repetition, where everything is ungodly, during the time of Sodom and Gomorrah, the ways of the world as we know it.

Look at how the government is doing things today. We're in a chemical warfare and people act like it's nothing. Society as a whole is so confused and nobody wants to speak up or try to do anything about the situation society faces. They're having a hard time getting the president out of office. There's something seriously wrong with that episode, wouldn't you say. The lower class people don't have a say on what goes on in this country.

Those are the people that built this country and keep it moving, as far as trade and labor; they're the livestock of this world. As of today, they're still slaves for the overseer and they're okay with it. That's why there are these different organizations, they all have one common interest and the government is part of at least some of them.

It's amazing how the government downplays it's involvement in affairs around the world. Like, for instance, the war on drugs. When there isn't really a war on drugs because this country needs those opiates for their pain narcotics, as well as the coca leaf--it's used as a stimulant--due to the fact that those plants won't grow in this part of the world. They have to trade for them, only because they're unable to produce it. They trade different countries for those products to process their medications.

This country uses a very large amount of opiates for different reasons; around 75 to 80 percent of the medications have some amount of opiate in them. Here's another reason that cocaine and heroin are illegal in this country, the government is unable to tax it.

As you see, they legalize marijuana now because it grows like tobacco and they can tax it. Outside the illegal acts that go on in the government, there are a lot of good things there as well. They supply good medical care for its society as a whole. Their socialism is pretty good, they supply a common ground with all members of society and try to have a better political movement for the community, rather than the individual.

They also all are working together, private individuals, to have a better relationship between the two parties, which are capitalism and communism. Here in this country, they centralize all economic planning for those in power.

Chapter 6

Also, according to the 13th and 14th Amendments of the United States Constitution, you have the right to be treated equally and fair for all parties. According to Congress. There's really nothing wrong with America, it's the people of America where the problems come from. Now, remember earlier I was talking about Capitol Hill, well one of the problems this country thought wasn't there any more is racism. Well, I come to pass that it's still here, it came out that there are a lot of racial injustices that are still going on in this country. It's back in the open. Now, let's take a look at all these hate crimes that are going on around this country. Especially those in Minneapolis, Washington D.C., Louisville, KY., and other places in this country. Hell, they can just bring the rope and start hanging the people of color again. Now, if that had been people of color, they would have been killed on site; those that were caught would be facing charges like anything from terrorism to treason to whatever else they could be charged with under the Federal law.

You know, a lot of the American people are afraid to challenge the law. They feel there isn't anything they can do. At some point, we as a people have to stand up for what's right according to the Law. It's funny because you can get together to destroy something, not to build something, and you want to talk about crazy. Now that's crazy. You'd rather kill than build. What's the logic in that?

The fundamentals about politics consist of being shrewd and suitable for the circumstances according to the situation. See, there's not one of you that is for the system they live in, but they tell you all these good lies about how they want to make things better for you. When they don't really give a damn about you.

Their main focus is on the upper class bracket. Here's a perfect example: you have been paying taxes all your life, now that the economy is suffering, the government doesn't really want to help the lowest tax brackets out. And the president says he wants to "Make America Great Again." Well, America wouldn't need to be made great again, had you all been doing the things to keep it great in the first place.

There are people losing their homes that they really don't own; you have these small businesses that have been crushed due to this pandemic that crippled the world and economically we are in dangerous times. It's very critical for society as a whole because it involves death and serious health problems. Then the government tells you they have it under control when the death rate is increasing greatly.

They say that to the people because the situation doesn't affect them. If you're not part of that upper class bracket, you're left out. They're trying to wait for you; then you're one less to think about, not that they are thinking about you. You also don't have to worry about converting to their party because you financially don't have the wealth. Now, there's some that finagle and manipulate by stealing and scheming, even cunning, which is common in our society.

The politicians have so many scandals that they expose to society until it isn't funny. They do that to satisfy the public. For their course of action, which is to manipulate the lower class bracket to believe that they're for you.

Now, there's some that right their wrongs and you have some that actually correct some of the problems, but man is so caught up on what they didn't do until they are unable to see they fix it. He's so worried about the things of the world.

Man is so caught up in the things of this world until it takes his heart from the creator who gave him life. By revealing this to you, I'm confident that you might be able to see how deceitful man can be. Furthermore, there is a greater evil among men. In order to be able to understand what the situation you're dealing with is, you must first step outside of the box to see your place. Then, and only then, will you be able to do your part.

Everyone of us has a role to play; play your part and let the next person do the same. Because there's nothing complicated about that. Understand that it's not all about man because he needs others to succeed. There is nothing man can do alone. That's why we're all users. You use me, I use them, and so on. Man was put here for a purpose and one of them is to love, as God loved him enough to give you life.

Man also has a responsibility to govern, teach, and council one another. Not to enslave man for his greed. It interferes with social realism among the lower class society. Keep in mind that one is no good without the other.

Man took the govern part to a level of being king and ruler and began to force man to do. That's where things began to get complicated among others.

That's one of the reasons for enslavement for control: you must remember even a tool has knowledge because destruction comes like a whirlwind and when your distress and anguish comes, you know that this too shall pass.

For life without struggle, man knows not, it's kind of like a battle; it has some form of superiority and that's where leadership comes into play.

Trust and believe and God will see you throughout, acknowledge Him in all your ways. And know that there's no way around being in bondage. It's a way of life as man knows it. Now that you know, that is half the battle.

So, yes there are injustices that we face everyday, but you have to deal with it. I know it's harder for some than others, but we all can relate.

We have these different supremacy groups that fuel their superiority which makes them superior over the underclass people; it has nothing to do with your ethnic background and we're all slaves. Because they have the power and means to do so.

Those people that are in power, it wasn't given to them, they took and made sacrifices to get that power to be in authority. What are you willing to do to get there? Because to some degree, they're in control but you still have the right to become sovereign, meaning, self-govern. By doing so, you're free from their laws and rules. Then you're free from bondage. Now, to claim sovereign, you would need to find somewhere to roam.

Because it's an old saying, in Rome you do as the Romans do or don't do. Then a lot of people don't know anything about sovereignty. Because all their lives they have been in bondage under some type of government. It's so impaired, the way their system treats people; it's immoral how they prey on others for their gain.

Most people don't know how much they're worth. If I were to ask someone how much they're worth, some would probably say nothing and others might say they can't be bought, but there's a price. Now if I told you that you are worth $999,999,999, what would you say? That's every 24 hours.

They came up with that figure because they use those nine digits that they identify you by and that's how they figure out your number daily.

Now, if you were able to figure out who holds your note, it becomes yours. You would have to claim your number. It's part of Wall Street, you're a stock and they're your broker. It's called the straw boss or straw man.

This is a major part of the bondage we live in today. Now, the government doesn't want you to know that because it would crash the stock market. Without that and the drug trade, this country would probably fall.

That's the life of this country, it's a part of the economy so see, without you there's no them. Crazy, hmm? Medically it's needed, as well as recreationally, using it to keep the money flowing around the world. Don't be that naive where you're unable to understand that those people that are in charge of the world only see you as a commodity or slave they can use for anything.

It's kind of like the story about King David where he killed a man because he felt he wasn't treating him right. So, he had him beheaded and now Saul was dead and his wife a widow. In society today you can't whip your chip because it's the law and if you break the law you will suffer the consequences.

A person's demeanor can be deceptive to the point that one could be tricked. The government is very deceitful because they have the power to do so; I want to be straightforward with you. It may seem like you're free to do any and everything you want. Okay, but there's a limit to what and when you can do those things, like there's a time for you to work, school, etc.

Also, there's a consequence for not doing as instructed. No matter how you view it, it's the law and the rules that were set for people to abide by. Actually in our social society, there's what's called accountability, which brings responsibility. And that means that whatever you're involved in, you're accountable for your part.

Throughout my life, I blamed people or the system for my actions. The rules and laws were designed for mankind to live by and if you think it doesn't apply to you, it does. They put it in effect to give order to man; they are for man to obey and when you don't, there are consequences for your actions. Really there's no one to blame but you. No one has control over you, so they monitor you, waiting for you to act against their rules so they can punish you. They already don't care for you so whenever you step out of line, they are there. Now, is that fair? I would have to say yes it is. Because you're responsible for you. You can't blame someone for what you're doing.

Now comes the trickery; out of all the presidents, this one is on a whole other level. I have never seen anything like that in my life and I'm sure you haven't either. Is that what you do when you don't want to step down? Now, see this president, one would assume he is very exceptional and this is his country.

Chapter 7

Being made aware of his superiority complex. He feels or thinks he's above the law and they don't apply to him and those of his status.

The racism he displays before the American people is really awful, for a man of his caliber you would not expect something like that to be exposed. It goes to show you what power is. Some people with power don't need it and he is one of them. He told his supporters that the election was stolen and then he held a rally and told them, "If you don't fight, then you're not American." He went on to say, "Let's walk down to Capitol Hill and show them America."

It's funny how the Republicans and those supremacy groups can get away with murder. Oh, it's okay, they're Americans, they did no wrong. Then you have the president sitting back and saying or doing anything about what's going around this country. Why? Maybe because he really doesn't care about the people or, if things aren't his way, then he doesn't want to have any part in it.

That's a bit selfish, don't you think? It's like do as I say and the way I say or else get away, I don't need you, type of deal. Now that America is in this big disarray behind his actions. The rest of the Republican party seem to fear him or won't go against him for that superior attitude they display. In a sense, he's worse than Hitler, because the American people are scared of him.

No one wants to admit that it's wrong and come together as a people. Instead, they prefer to sit back and act like adolescents. Like all these racially discriminated episodes that are taking place due to his leadership and the American people get away with it.

Then to allow for those white supremacy groups riots on Capitol Hill that caused a destruction in Washington D.C. for the sake of white power. Now, who's to blame for that madness happening on Capitol Hill? I guess no one. Now, does that define America, the trade center of the world? Acting like savages or barbarians, carrying on like uncivilized citizens. That's so inhumane for this society to produce such a sadistic tactic; don't people have any concern for others or are they all just evil inside?

The barbarian culture believes they're inferior to other people, they cruelly possess a dominant and supreme attitude toward the people. Somewhat like Trump, with his rudeness and the cruelty he displays is that of hate, even though he fears being corrected for his wrongs and acts like nothing happened; it shows that he has no concern for this country and what it's supposed to stand for.

If it's not Donald's way, it's no way. Kind of like if you ain't on what I'm on, you get shit on. Then when he executes his power to control the American people seem shocked.

Remind you that you all gave him the authority by voting him into office. I know it's complicated for some but for others, they're okay with it because it falls up under white power and their superiority complex, which gives them the entitlement as a people. Since, after all, the people made him lord and ruler. Even with him out of office, you still have the problem, because who's next? Because someone has to be in charge, wouldn't you say there's no satisfaction for the people.

Life is about sacrifices; in order to become successful, a person has to be willing to make a sacrifice in order to accomplish their goals or whatever they seek to acquire in life.

At what price are you willing to pay for your success? Ask yourself, "Is it all or nothing?" Whatever decision you make, accept whatever comes from that choice.

At some point you have to stop and think about what direction you want to go in and whatever choice you make about your situation, accept it and move on. When it comes to society, there's a lot of people in the world and it's hard to keep up with them.

You're either the predator or the prey; that really determines the outcome of your life.

This is why you have people to somewhat make decisions for the people as whole. They're put there to oversee a certain area or groups. When it becomes unmanageable, they ask for some assistance from other sources.

They get together and come up with a solution for whatever the situation may be. Now, by doing that, figure if it works here then we can use it abroad. They create the poison to destroy a population of people worldwide and give it a name like AIDS, HIV, or coronavirus and then spread it. Now, as they are dispensing it, they can begin to maintain control of the situation.

These people are playing with our lives, which in essence, they're the puppet master and we're the puppets and there's nothing we can do about it. Isn't that something? Do you like being demoralized by the government because we are at their disposal and there's nothing we can do about it.

Take those people in prison, they're considered worthless, nothing, nobodies, and slaves; not to say they don't deserve to be there, but to be treated like animals is wrong. I'm sure everyone has done something against the law, you're already in bondage so why enslave a person any more; it's part of capitalism.

Prison is one of the biggest subjects in the world and the people are alright with it. Prison is not only physical, it affects the mental state as well.

A person has to condition themself to be able to deal with it psychologically. Being in a limited to small area with time to eat, work, shower, and recreate, as well as have visits from family and friends. Let's not get it confused; it causes a mental disorder. There's evidence that proves when a person is put in an enclosed area that becomes their new normal, to take them from that area they don't know how to respond to that environment. That's because you took them from their safe zone. Now with people being confined for 15 to 20 years, they don't know anything about society outside of prison. The success rate of those that stay out is a ration of two out of ten will not return to prison. Why, because that person is what's known as institutionalized and if released will commit another crime to go back to prison. Society outside of prison is strange to them.

All that don't commit suicide will be in prison, that's the only life they know. That's suitable for society, this is only a few of the examples that happen. Then you have those that can't take being locked up and commit suicide. There are all kinds of different excuses as to why the system locks you away and deems you unfit for society. It's horrifying, the way they treat people while they're incarcerated. It's lonely on the inside, especially when they have no one on the outside with support. Just imagine being in a state hospital where they medicate you with those psychotic drugs and label you as insane, that becomes home for you. It's just like you getting a life sentence without parole. So, see, this bondage thing is a very serious event in our society and without it, I could only imagine what it would be like for mankind.

Realistically, who's to say what's right and what's wrong because what is right for one person could be wrong for the next person. The same with good and bad. Here's where the government comes into play. The overseer makes the law and you are to follow them and for those of you that don't, there's a consequence for not obeying the law.

I would imagine that is why some of you don't see it as bondage. You don't want to believe that it even exists anymore. You don't want to believe people are being sold into slavery. In some countries, women and girls are sold into prostitution. Here in America, it happens, but not a lot. Now here they have what's called the pimp association, and Las Vegas is where it's legal but it does exist.

Society might want to continue to be naive but that's okay. Now maybe you can help society understand how this government can allow the American people to be terrorized by these white supremacy groups, like Proud Boys and Q-Anon, that display racism and do nothing. So, what do the people do? Nothing, I would have to guess. Nothing, just accept it and keep moving on because one man's failure is another man's glory.

A person must understand that this country is run by a government and they say what you can or cannot have or do. The majority is white here and that's what gives them the power to control society as a whole. You can make believe that it's not true but they would only be insane to think like that.

Providing you don't have any form of capital or wealth, then you're just a nobody, no matter what ethnic group it is. Everyone has their own views and opinions about things involving society. It would be safe to say we can all come to a common ground. That we have to abide by their rules.

Question, have you ever felt trapped or caged? Well, that's what it feels like being enslaved. There's not much freedom and there's no such thing as free; just because you're able to move around freely doesn't mean you're free, because you're only allowed to do so much. Some of you would say, "Well what am I, if I'm not free?" You are in bondage.

The main point and purpose for the government is to control the surroundings and put people in a place to oversee them and the area they want to conquer.

This system is not for the poor, they're just a tool that they use to get things done. This world is so corrupt until it isn't funny. However, they can convince you they will. It's amazing how the people that come from other countries and apply for citizenship once they get their green card, they don't have to pay taxes for the first five years they're here and they get what you can't, like business loans and housing. They also tell them not to trust the African-American, he's the worst of all and can't be trusted. The government is a department of separated people from all over the world. The American man is cross bred with different ethnic groups from around the world. There is no land of the free, but they tell you it is. Sure, for who? Yes, it's better than those third world countries, but we're living in a time where the world is a disaster, with this virus that's killing people by the thousands daily and the American government is unable to get a handle on it. It's weird how the president tried to downplay it and would tell the American people about it many months after this country was exposed to it, come to find out they had already planned this years before it happened. The American government blames China for the virus. It's hard to believe because the news talked about the pandemic in 2008 and in 2010 they were working on a vaccine for the virus.

Under population control gives them the right to allow who they want to do whatever they want to do. This said group of people that's in charge of a certain area, they sit down and discuss what they want to do and then do it. They differentiate between the people as to who does what and when, not to discredit anyone from the project. Remember me saying everyone has a part to play, when it's your turn then you do your part. No more or less is required.

Now, let's get back to the late 60s and 70s when they put this experiment with alcohol into the black community; they put a liquor store onto every other corner to intoxicate all the blacks. One of their thoughts was to keep them drunk and we can control them. That didn't work so well for them.

Now it's time for another session to discuss what else we can do to slow that group of people down to be able to monitor them. So after the war,the heroin epidemic hit America and a lot of the soldiers came back with a habit, so they decided to flood the black community with heroin, hoping to kill them off and overdose. It's helped some, not like they intended to.

Moving forward to the 80s, they introduced cocaine to the system and it was said it was a rich man's drug. When it hit the black community, they were amazed by it. It started to take over different communities and it kept spreading until the 90s, by this time it had hit the mayor's door. He started complaining to the senator and it went on up the chain. By the mid-90s, it hit the White House and now little rich kids had to come to the hood to scrounge up the drugs. Lille, Johnny, and Brecky taking the gold eating utensils to support their addiction.

It's amazing how it went from the ghetto to the White House. Now it's a problem only because it hit home, their plan backfired. How, you don't need to be locked up; you need treatment for your addiction.

In today's society, if you commit a crime and it's drug-related, you don't go to jail, you get treatment. When the governor's daughter became an addict is when we have a war on drugs. It wasn't a problem as long as it was in the ghetto, but once it hit the upper class white people, it became a major problem. They're the European native descendants who have always been trying to rule over Black native tribes, long ago with the different ethnic nationality. Need I remind you that there are different types of bondages, those are only a few of the hidden tales of the world.

It's reality and you can not do anything about the situation you face everyday. America is so full of turmoil, this nation is at an unrest state of being, dealing with all that's going on in the world. It's a critical time for the American people, due to this white supremacy, COVID-19, and the other crises this country suffers from. There's so much happening and before they can get one situation under control, there's another crisis just as bad, if not worse. American society is always at a loss, even when you're winning you're still at a loss. This system wasn't designed for the poor to win. But they tell you they have it under control, knowing they're lying and then cover a lie with another lie.

These are the people you voted for.

The society that we live in was designed only for the wealthy, they're the only ones that really benefit from this tragedy we are suffering from in America. It doesn't affect them because they can afford it. Now, there's a part of society that's not talked about and that's the drug addicts and prisoners.

They both suffer a severe enslavement. And society doesn't want to have anything to do with them as a whole. They don't publically speak on those issues as much. Why? Is it because society looks down on them. I would imagine that you see them as worthless, unfit, and losers. I believe that a lot of people in society feel that they don't have to accept them because they're not a part of your society. Well, you're wrong, they are a part of society as a whole. Mainly because all of the taxpayers are supporting them. On top of that, it's a multi-trillion dollar stock on Wall Street. But to them, you're a nobody until it hits home and then it's a different view because now they have some in the same situation. Now, that's another form of bondage because those people have someone they care about, now they're suffering just like the addicts or those that are in prison. There's a variety of types of bondage that I can validate based on experience. Then you have those that have a family member who's addicted to drugs or in prison and it causes them to break down. Now, they're on antidepressants or some went to alcohol and there are some who just couldn't handle it and committed suicide.

You know that depression is a mental form of bondage, it causes sadness, fear, and loneliness. They figure if I can't get you this way, I'll get you another.

Not being able to interact with loved ones, being deprived of your freedom due to things that happen. That drug addict is locked up in their addiction and it's hard for their family and friends to see them suffer or be locked up. Well, for a lot of you, you probably can't or aren't able to relate to what's happening around you. Mainly because it isn't you.

By America being the trade center of the world. They have the need to be at the head of all trades. Which I think is a good thing because it keeps America in the loop. This is a good country and there are some good people. Everybody isn't corrupt or heartless. Out of all the countries in the world, I don't think there's anywhere I'd rather be except here.

This is actually a great country compared to some of those third world countries they show and talk about. No matter where you're at or go, there's always some positives and negatives; they go together because if everything was always good, then there would be no bad. I'm sure it's like that all over the world. Everybody isn't selfish or greedy. Most of the country is in good shape mentally and physically. This work force here is very good for the most part. Some states have more jobs than others, but it balances out.

Most of the major cities have a high crisis of homeless people, it's been like that for years. It's a few things I know about America, it's a very diplomatic community; there are people from all over the world here.

This country isn't prejudiced when it comes to people, there's a place for all people of the world here.

It's weird, the way this government operates, they don't care about the other party as long as they get what they want or need from them.

I'm only saying from a political view, it seems that the way to get things done is by doing things on their level, that is the way to function. They have a guideline for you to follow. Now if you follow that, then you can make it.

In accordance with the laws, bi-laws, and policies, they're to live under considering all of that, whether you agree or disagree, they were made for people to abide by. Well, we know everyone is not going to do so and for those people, that's their choice and they have to deal with the outcome.

I am unsure about how you view this world or this country and what goes on. I do understand that there's nothing I can do to change anything, but I am willing to try, with the help of others; what about you? Now, I am able to empathize with some of you because we suffer from some of the same issues. Not to downplay anyone, because everyone is important and of value, but to what length are you willing to go to for what you believe in? At the end of the day, it isn't about me, it's about you! At what point do you stop blaming others for your actions?

Especially when it comes to authority, most don't have any, but you're not alone, around 70% of the world don't. I ask myself is this all part of God's plan for man and, if so, what did man do to deserve this punishment?

Then again, I said Jesus was tortured, tormented, and killed for doing what was good and right. Then I had to go back to Adam and Eve.

So, I ask, how long does man have to suffer for the deeds of others?

I'm sure everyone knows that this is man's world. And there is a standard you must live by, which is the law. Now, you say it ain't fair, but what is fair according to the law. There's two types of justice: one for the elite and one for the non-elite; keep in mind that as a minority, the law is for you, not them. The scale is not level. They can justify to show they're right according to the reason, now you, on the other hand, you're unable to do so. So, as long as you stay within your rim, you're alright.

They're not all to blame for why we're still in bondage, or should I say suffering? We are more dangerous to ourselves than they are to us. At least they made it to where you are able to be successful, it's not really them that keeps us down, it's your own people. It's sad that I don't want you to be successful, now, why that is, I don't know.

I can say out of all the different ethnic groups, the African-Americans are the only people that I witness don't want to see one elevated above them. It's sad but it's the truth. Personally, I think that a person should be able to rise to the top and to do that help is needed.

Most cultures work together and work from the bottom to the top and everyone that came from the bottom to the top go back and help the next person get there.

It's not in the African-American culture to do that; one of them gets there and they're done, they don't care if you make it or not, so, to me, they're worse than those in power. They won't come back to help anyone else get out or to have a better life. It's not like they're obligated to, but they know what it's like to live in poverty.

Chapter 8

It's not going to be easy to get ahead, you have to be determined and stay focused and you can't be afraid to give up something just to get something. To get to where you're in the upper class bracket, you have to be willing to sacrifice something to be successful. I would say about 80% of the people who are wealthy weren't born wealthy. They had to do whatever it took to get there and they're willing to do that much more to stay there. So keep in mind that winners don't quit and quitters don't win. There's an old saying, the game is cold, but it's fair; a hep see, only a few know many are called and only a few are chosen. And I go on to say, the game is also to be sold and not told.

Those people that become rulers, they get there by being nice. That's why it's important to understand why there is bondage in the world.

We are put in different situations for different reasons. I believe it's to challenge your behavior or to see what your limits are, either way point being, is to see how you react to the situation you face.

We are living in a very chaotic time around the world and our society is at its breaking point. How do we as a people get through?

Well, as I said earlier, by using each other to stand together as a nation and not a people. Sure, we're in bondage, but by working together as a team, we can win. The whole world looks at America as the leader of the world. Why? Because we are from all over the world in one country, trying to make the world a better place.

All I am doing is lowering the cover so society can see and understand the world we live in. That's why there's a poverty line, it consists of people or families that fall below the classification of being poor according to the government. For many that's the only life they know and they're okay with that. Now, let's say we took a wealthy family and put them in poverty without the wealth. What do you think would happen to that family? Nine out of ten they wouldn't survive. Right now, we have some well off people going to the food shelter for food due to the COVID-19 crisis. They're not used to that but they have to eat. Now, we're talking about the people that thought they never would have crashed and gave up on life, even killing themselves to keep from living without, after being in that wealthy group of lifestyles.

This crisis that the world suffers from has gotten the attention of people all over the world. I'm almost sure that there were some that were unable to take it, being in this epidemic that our government calls a pandemic. Because they refused to deal with it and ended their life.

Now for others, it's an eye opener to reality, by letting the upper class people of society experience how it is being without food or being able to pay your mortgage or car note. I'm sure that not anyone likes what's going on but, at the same time, maybe those have to compare with those that don't can finally be able to understand the struggle the underclass people go through and just maybe, they can appreciate not having to worry about food or a place to live. Your mental concept is damaged, you're stressed out, and your anxiety levels are at an all time high.

Not knowing what to expect next due to your current situation and not knowing how to escape from this madness. You feel entangled, you're unsure of your situation at this point. When it seems like all and everything has failed, you can always call on God or whoever you believe is your savior.

Well, some of you have never had to figure out where you were going to sleep for the night or where or when your next meal would be. Now during this time, some of you are able to empathize with the people that don't have anything. I know this subject isn't talked about because no one wants to discuss this issue. They know that our society doesn't have enough jobs for the people to work or housing for the people to live in, so what do they do? They avoid the situation altogether. The government becomes neutral and leaves it for society to figure out. Nevertheless, people pay all these different taxes, and for what.

There's land tax, property tax, sales tax, worker tax, state and federal taxes, don't forget about city and county taxes as well. What about the people in these cities, counties, and states who need help, where do they go? Most working people find it hard for them to pay their mortgages, due to them not making the cost of living from their job. So the average working family makes about 55 to 60 thousand a year, combined, and they have two children, so they're at poverty level according to society. You wonder why the crime rate is up. It's at an all time high because the state you live in doesn't want to put back some of that tax money they took or force you to pay.

People have responsibilities and their wages don't cover their cost of living in the state.

Now more than ever the American economy is down, about 65% of the American people don't have a job due to this coronavirus; right now there's about nearly 4,000 people dying every day and the government doesn't really care.

They claim they have a vaccine for it but won't dispense it to the American people. They would rather go to Europe or somewhere else. They have people here that need to be vaccinated and then they don't dispense enough to the people to get dosed. This is generally all done by those you put in charge of this country.

Now that puts people at risk, so now their survival skills come into effect. What's to be expected in a crisis like this where you don't know if you catch it you live or die or how long you will be affected by it.

There's different ways to examine this situation. Let's be real, it's not good. There is nothing the citizens can do about the problem America faces. Now there's those exceptional people that don't really give a damn because they're not affected by the pandemic. There are many effects due to all the problems it has caused for people all over the world.

This will never be forgotten. It's like that Hitler episode where he tried to kill all of the Jewish people off. And there are actually some people that's alright within America. America has problems like any other country. Every country does different things. People from other countries talk about the good, as well as the bad. America is not perfect. Far from it.

It's fascinating how the system is designed, it's like you never get ahead because the government always has loopholes to prevent it, stall, etc.

It's standard for a person to work and pay taxes. Now if you don't have any credit you can't get any. This country was built on bartering, that's when a man's word meant something, but as time moves forward, it's changed. Now if you don't have the money or something of value, you're part of the underclass people.

They put up this front like a small business loan to start your own business, now when you apply for one, most people get turned down for one reason or another.

Don't take what I'm saying the wrong way, some do get that loan they needed or a co-signer.

Well, I'm kind of what's called a compassionate person and I'm sure I'm not alone. I was raised in the South, back then those people stuck together because that's all they had, each other. So, they did for one another, now, most of them were what's called a sharecropper. Lots of them lived on farmland and they worked the land. Especially those people of color. Today there's no unity nor compassion for people. Everyone is always complaining about what they don't like, but what are you willing to do about it?

As you can see, what the government thinks about the people. They really don't give a damn about you because if they did, they wouldn't be killing you off. We are under a chemical warfare and most of America is too blind to see what's happening. It's awful that no one is willing to address the problem America faces. Everybody is relying on the government to take care of all the killing that's going on. Then when they feel enough lives have been taken worldwide and not before.

I was instructed to write this book to share my view about what's going on around the world. Time is running out for all that's seeking forgiveness for your wrong, now is the time to seek it from the father of man. Not to imply that you have to be holier than thou, just be right by self and others and learn to love one another as God loves you.

As you go through life, you learn that we all have different experiences and learn from them. Through my life, I've learned that it's easier to be kind to others than hateful towards people. I would like to encourage you to practice doing at least one good deed every day. It will help release some of that mental bondage you live with everyday.

The transformation has to start somewhere and during your transient, do some good because no one knows when they are leaving this life. There's nothing we can do to stop it. You don't have to feel trapped or powerless due to the circumstances we live under, it's all a part of life.

Do what you can and the good Lord will do the rest. Remember it's not our way, it's His way. I believe that God has a way of making things known to man, all you have to do is pay attention to the signs that are given. A lot of things that happen are predestined and those things just accept and move forward. You have to understand that you're not in control. For some, you have to go through the suffering in order to appreciate your blessings.

I want to leave this with you: the things that you go through in this life is preparing you for the life to come. Know that whatever you have done, seen, and been through, those were before experiencing that, too. Keep in mind there's a place and time for everything under the sun.

I would like to take this time to thank God for this opportunity to share my views on life in which we live. I've been a slave to man. Now, I'm willing to be a slave for God because being a slave for man really sucks. There's only so much that can be done to man before he breaks, once he's mentally broken. He's no good to society as a whole and in some cases he loses his comprehension or becomes a threat to society. Then when either of those things happen, they lock you away from society as a whole and deem you unfit for society. Once they put that label on you, "psychopath" or "criminal," it's over. The system fears what it cannot control. Regardless of who or what it is. One of the codes they live by is kill or be killed, that's what gives them control. That's why a person must be willing to offer or make sacrifices to be of that status.

It's a part of, now, what are you willing to do for your success or future? Are you willing to become undomesticated, vicious, or uncivil to mankind for the power to control or be part of those who have the power? In order to associate with that group, you must be like them or be of some type of value to them.

Having restrictions is part of bondage, it's not a bad thing to have limitations and stipulations on what you can and cannot do or have. With the respect of others, you follow the plan or you can be disobedient and suffer the consequences for your actions. Then it's like you're an outcast so the elimination comes into play. They don't like to be challenged.

Because they're competitive and they don't like any complications and you're of no value. It's kind of like being the president and losing all your power.

The only difference is when you strip one of them of their authority, their self-worth falls with them and they find out it's lonely at the bottom. Most of them kill themselves because of the shame and disappointment of being a failure. The mental pressure is too great for them.

It wouldn't surprise me if our last president tried to kill himself behind losing his power or fear of going to prison. You know, he is one of them that thinks he's smarter than the US government. As they say, what you put in the washer will come out in the ringer. I have done some stupid things in my life and I'm sure some of you have as well, but how stupid is it to tell the United States government you're smarter than them because you only paid $750.00 in taxes for the past ten years or so? Is that why he wanted a pardon before he left office? Maybe he feels like he's exempt from prosecution. Because he was the President of the United States.

Now, see this is how those in power see things. They can wipe out a country or a nation of people and get away with it. Now, you, on the other hand, can rob a store and get 30 years in prison. That's crazy but it's the truth and they say it's justice.

The law should apply the same for everyone that commits a crime. In America, it doesn't. There's some who might agree and some will disagree, either way it's fine; approximately 80% of the wealthy would be okay with the way things are because the law doesn't apply to them. Plus, they don't get prosecuted; now, for the lower class people, just about whatever crime they commit, they can lock you up away from society. Why is that? Where is the equal justice? Well, when it comes down to crime, our society weighs things differently when it comes to what type of crime, who commited the crime, and where the people who commited the crime are. At least this in this country it is. Depending on your ethnicity determines the outcome. Now, is that fair or should I say along with the bracket you're in? The wealthy, they're more favored than any other bracket.

My opinion is if you send one person to prison and the other committed a crime, they should go to prison as well; it shouldn't have anything to do with your ethnicity or whether you're wealthy or not. Because they both broke the law.

I'm not against the law, I just don't understand the difference between the way they apply the law when it comes to who goes to jail and who goes home.

I do know that the lower class people are from the high class people. Especially if they have the same crime. I'm sure I am not the only person who feels like that but these are the issues we face in our society. No one seems to give a damn about the minorities; they're the people who don't matter.

They want to talk about how great America is, well what about how bad it is? That's not talked about. They don't talk about how the government flooded the African-American community with guns and drugs to kill off the black society.

Chapter 9

Only it actually didn't work out like they expected. Back when I was a child, there were no teenagers buying 50 kilograms of cocaine or heroin like there are today. What's so great about that, you tell me, because I really want to know and I'm sure there are more people who feel the same. What happened to our society? I am sure some of you can remember the white children were not allowed to act with the black children that much. Now, after that major drug epidemic hit, Brecky Sue was hooked on heroin and the only way for her to get drugs without her parents knowing was to go deal with the negro, that's what they called the black people back in that time. Time has changed in some aspects, but not much. Society is as prejudiced as it was, but there are more interactions with the different ethnic groups of people and that's a good thing. Now, if we can just get from under the racism in this country. I know it's a difficult project, being that it involves capital and it's not just one set of people involved, so that probably won't ever happen.

Bring to mind Wall Street is where you'll find racism because 85% of those people are very wealthy and interact with the people of the world. That has power to control some part of the stock market you would say. They're a different league from the middle class league. Those are the elite crowd, who are in charge of the world. Most politicians are investors to be able to stay on track with what's of value. Being a part of that particular crowd gives one an edge socially. It's not about races, it's about commodities. America is the trading post.

Everything has a price and everything is for sale. There's a lot of uneducated people of color in society, mainly because the elders have no time for them. We live in a society where babies are having babies and the baby doesn't know anything because their parents weren't there to raise them or they don't go to school.

Why, because there's nobody there to force or tell them they must go to school. Mainly because the fathers are not in the child's life because he's either a drug addict or criminal and the mother is too busy hanging out or using drugs. So, that leaves those children alone and society is left to raise that child. Don't get it confused, all of society isn't like that, but there's a large population that suffers from that abandonment. It's not that child's fault and those children don't deserve that. This is a vicious cycle we live in. No one seems to care about the young people. Everybody is so caught up on the jones until they lose focus on reality. A lot of the parents are so confused until they forget what's a priority. This is what happens when you let society raise your children. Those children suffer from neglect, abuse, and not knowing their parents. It's the parent's responsibility to be there in that child's life. Everyone is in a hurry to do nothing. It's not that child's fault you're not there. I am guilty of that. I allowed myself to be misled by the fame and what was going on in the street life until it took control of my life, which caused my child to be without her father. And drugs and alcohol play a major part in people's choices. You wonder why those children are so rebellious towards their parents and other adults. I get it, they need to blame something or somebody for what's happening in your life. Now, I would say to stop blaming and get yourself back on track; you still have a chance to do something different. Like being a part of that child's life, if possible. You can't change the past but you can work for a better future because you both need to know each other.

Don't blame that child because it's not that child's fault you weren't there. We're always looking for the easy way out, but there's no easy way out of this situation; you chose not to be there. Because whatever you were doing was more important than your child. I know things happen and each situation is different, the severity of a drug addiction can cause abandonment, but it shouldn't because that's not the main issue, it's something else that causes the separation.

I know it's very hard to be in a child's life if one of the parents is in a different state or even in prison and all of that comes with choices. Now there are some people that have children and just choose not to be there and then others are so caught up in that certain type of lifestyle to where or what they're doing may be harmful for that child, which will separate them for the safety of the child. That child still didn't deserve not having their parents in their life, for whatever reason, if they're alive. I can not blame anyone for the choices I made, especially when it comes to my child. She should have been the most important thing in my life, but she wasn't. I thought I was doing something right at the time because I was part of an organization and my life was so chaotic. So, I thought I was doing the right thing but I wasn't because my child should have been first and I should have let nothing interfere with that. Remember it early that at what point do you take responsibility for your actions? Well for me, it's now.

She did not deserve my absence and no child does, so, for the parents reading this, your child needs both parents in their life.

Over the years, the American people thought that racism was gone and this country had moved on. Until the white supremacists came out of hiding when the president wasn't being re-elected so they had to let society know that they still existed and an injustice took place because they were Trump supporters.

Now the American people were fooled because for years there had not been any racial crimes happening, but in 2020, they surfaced with all these lynchings that took place where those of the elite crowd felt they had to show the American people who was in charge. Now when those extremists attacked Capitol Hill, who would have thought something like that would have happened behind an election?

Now, President Trump and his extremists have shaken America and I'm willing to bet that Trump will be excluded from that attack. Then that only shows who is in power. This country suffers from a great discrimination due to the leadership of this country. Most people don't want to face the reality that racism still exists in America, no matter how they try to cover it up, it's there.

I want to say that this is the only country in the world where the African-Americans are still not accepted or equal to other racial groups in this country.

Here in America, they play the shell game where you put the pea under one of the three shells and pick which one, knowing it's not under either; it's trickery.

I can only talk about America because it's the only country I know anything about. Considering the way the government does things. There's always a conspiracy going on. They don't really care about the people, they only care about how they can use you to benefit them. The people that are in charge are more worried about some other country and what they can do for them.

When there's a lot wrong with this country. They rather go to Iran or Iraq and get into affairs than go to get America in order. This country suffers from a lot of things like unemployment, homeslessness, and even sickness.

You think they care? The poverty level is very high in this country due to the government's lack of concern for the American people. They say this is the land of the free, proud, and brave. Well, it isn't free and I don't know why they're proud.

Now here's what the United States did: they created, along with others, these different kinds of diseases like AIDS, HIV, and COVID-19 to infect the world for control. They took countries like Kenya and other third world countries and exposed those countries to these diseases they created for population control. Now there's different types that come from different countries.

See, they're all in it together to maintain control. When it comes to this pandemic, they claim to have different types of strains that come from other countries. Not to say they don't exist but, for the most part, I would have to say it's a hoax. It's like they sent out this message that deadly diseases are killing all over the world, but not telling you they created it. Then they lead society on an illusion that they're working on a cure for it. They want society to get in an uproar but not to panic. It's to put fear in society to be able to continue to have control. This is part of how the government operates worldwide.

They are the oppressor and it's not optional for society as a whole to be involved. It's all part of the psychological behavior that they use to manipulate society into bondage. It's all about trickery and deception.

For a while I was fooled by their actions, then I asked why it was only affecting the lower class part of society. It's not affecting the wealthy upper class that much.

There's something wrong with this episode, wouldn't you think. There is a serious function that's going on when the government doesn't take serious action against an extremist group that attacks the government. Oh. That's right. They're a part of a white supremacist group and it's alright.

I find that overwhelming because they're white and so it's alright for them to attack the government. They are above the law, not because they're wealthy, only because they're white Republicans, on top of displaying racism. Had that been any other ethnic group of people, most of them would have been dead and the rest of them would be in prison for 20-to-life. And society is alright with it. When it comes to racism, it's not all about one ethnic group of people because they're people from different ethnic groups that are part of the government and they did as they were told. Which was to stand down.

There are so many injustices going on in this country, there's a great social disfunction that causes discrimination among society. There is too much going on in this country and it seems like no one cares to stand or say or do anything about what's happening.

So, they want to diverge from the situation America faces. Which, to me, is a cowardly act on the government's behalf. The rest of the world looks up to America.

Chapter 10

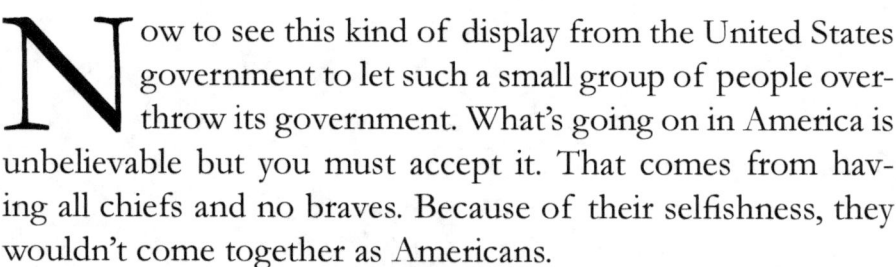

Now to see this kind of display from the United States government to let such a small group of people overthrow its government. What's going on in America is unbelievable but you must accept it. That comes from having all chiefs and no braves. Because of their selfishness, they wouldn't come together as Americans.

And we're supposed to be an example to the world, being that this is the trade center of the world. Behind this racism, we're losing respect around the world, where's the dignity in that. They talk about Making America Great Again.

Well, maybe I'm missing something, but from where I stand there's little respect for humans in America. Everything that's going on in the world today America has a part in. Yes, I know that there are oppressors all over the world, but there has got to be a breaking point or we can continue to be okay with our situation. It's just something to think about.

Those that are wealthy are not concerned about what's going on in this country. Now take these African-American movie stars and NBA/NFL/MLB athletes that once lived in poverty but now they're in a different class. How many do you think really care about your struggle. I have relatives that are wealthy and do you think they care or are concerned about their family members? I'm happy for them, they made it out of the ghetto. I hear people talk about it, "If I was rich, I'd do this or that for my community." Most say that but it doesn't happen. My mother told me, she said, "One penny of your means or then 50 million of somebody else." And she's right because that penny is mine and I can do whatever I want to with it. It's the same with them, it's theirs.

With some money they make them and others they make the money. Now the ones that are caught up on the money are very dangerous because they will do whatever it takes to get it and that much more to keep it.

We are in the devil's playground and you should already know the society we live in is selfish and only concerned with itself. Which they're not by themself.

Now, being that we're all users, you necessarily need to misuse or abuse others to get what you need or want to have. It's that superior attitude that makes you feel or seem bigger or better than the next person which, in your mind, you think you're in control. Ever since entitlement came about, people feel they're entitled to treat people like slaves and then people became okay with their entitlement, which is why we are in bondage of today.

Does it ever stop? Probably not because over the centuries of man, it's been that way and it's still that way. Yes, there are some people out there for the good of the people and all of the leaders aren't selfish or cruel people. There must be rules for men to live by and that's alright. To physically enslave a human being, I think it's wrong from my view, now some may think otherwise.

A person must have a strong mind frame in order to deal with this racism that's continued to go on in America, it has become outrageous in today's society.

The way people are still being treated cruelly and beaten, as well as killed, for the sake of greed. This is a mean world we live in and some things won't ever change. Now, when I was little, the whites treated the blacks so badly, but if you worked for them they would put up with it. There weren't any blacks allowed to go in the front door. And you had to say mister or missus or yes sir, boss sir. That's a different time from now.

Over the years of my life, I've witnessed a lot of tragedy along the way, some more worse than others. Man's life today is worth next to nothing.

We are all users, we need each other to get things done and that's okay, but to prey on the weak, I believe that it is wrong to prey on people for your greed or the need to be in power. With that in mind, we all have beliefs, views, and opinions.

It's okay to agree to disagree, as well as it's okay to disagree to agree. Because we all have that in common. At what point do you say enough is enough and come together and say something needs to change in society as a whole.

It doesn't seem like protesting is doing any good; our people are still being killed and treated unfairly. They say you have rights, what rights does one have because at the end of the day, you're still in bondage. No matter what we do or say, we still don't have the power to change or make a difference in society.

In the political world, you're either a shark or a fish. Because you have the Republicans, Democrats, Independents, and the liberals, which are one in the same. Meaning they're in power and, due to your status, your voice doesn't mean anything.

It's all about power; the Republicans vs. Democrats are fighting for control when it's not really a big deal because in the end, they're still the same. This is why they change every four to eight years, because the lower class doesn't meet their status.

They continue to fill society with all these lies and we believe them; what happened to that saying, "United we stand, divided we fall"?

We're in this pandemic that's killing people by the thousands daily.

What's the government doing about that? Nothing. They put up a good front.

You and I both know that it doesn't apply to the lower class people. They're all alone in their struggle of life as they know it. I specifically want you to understand that the system wasn't designed for the poor or lower class people. It is for them to impose on the lower class. They live by a code: I'm master and you slave. They feel the only thing you're worth is to keep them wealthy. They figure your sole purpose it to serve them.

As centuries pass, things have changed. Now, they need you to survive because it's the lower class people that keep society going. Because we are their slaves and whatever we make we give it right back to them. It's really a two-way street and you only get the scraps. Now, some of you get above the poverty level and do well and seem to forget where you came from and say, "I got mine, they better get theirs." Now, for those that give back or reach out to those they left behind, I want you to know it gets lonely on top. Now that you're there, are you willing to do what it takes to stay there? It becomes a duty to be willing to make a sacrifice of something of value to belong in that society; are you willing to pay that price for your success? Nothing is for free. So keep in mind what you view as just and unjust because you are responsible for your actions.

Just remember: it's no fun when you're all alone. Consequently, it doesn't only apply to the whites because there are white people that are treated like the blacks, only they call them white trash. And the wealthy look down on them.

We are dealing with this big democracy in this country that allows racial discrimination that's so destructive to the welfares of the people. It's very disgraceful and disrespectful to the American people who built this country.

People of the world might not want to deal with America behind their poor leadership. It's a civil war, the way this country is acting out with each other over control. They must have forgotten that America was built by immigrants. So why is it so hard for the American people to live together without fear or being oppressed by those that are supposed to be in charge?

This is what happens when you elect people to be in power; they lose focus and become power struck, without any concern for the people.

This is why there are groups like the KKK, Proud Boys, Q-Anon, neo-Nazis, Black Panther, and other militant groups in our society. Their main focus is hate and the sense of superiority over the next group of people.

The world we live in is scary. You don't know what to expect next because everyone is a target. So, who do you trust? I would have to say no one.

I can remember when you didn't have to lock your doors and the children were allowed to go out and play and you didn't have to worry about them being kidnapped. Now you have to hold onto your child because you have all these different people out there waiting for the right moment to snatch up the child. I understand your fear.

Those are just some of the things that are going on and they think it's alright to do it. It's not right to terrorize people or have them living in fear. It's sad but it happens all over the world. And a lot of it is for money and power.

Where is the justice? There is no justice, it's their way or else. So, the people are under their control and, depending on what you do, there are different types of punishment that you receive for that act you did against that person. Anything from being beaten to death is that person's punishment and society is alright with it. It's funny, but depending on who you are determines the outcome of the situation at hand.

Now, take the latest president, for his actions against the American government; him and his group of white supremacists, for the excitement of a riot, most of them are probably going to get probation and maybe a few of them will get prison time. Now when it comes to him, probably nothing will happen to him, but he won't be able to hold office in the government again.

It will be a surprise to the American people if he receives any type of punishment. Which, in fact, he should be charged with something like treason or attack on the American government, but then again he is one of the people that are in the crowd, unlike you or me, we're nobodies. We are like a pawn on the chessboard, expendable; in other words, worthless. They use us as puppets and cast us to the wolves to be eaten. That's what happens to slaves. They use you until they can't use you anymore, then dispose of you like trash. You become useless to them and anything or anybody they can't benefit from becomes disposable. So see, the government uses people to better themselves and once they have used you, they dispose of you because you're no longer needed; you become a sacrifice for their greater good. Now, as for the saying, "By the People, for the People," it's a bunch of crap.

The politicians tell all these different lies about they care for you, knowing it's a lie, but you believe them, hoping they do some of the things they said. Because you need to believe in something, so who if not them? And when they don't follow through, you say something like, "I knew that was going to happen."

You're really not free, they will tell you what to do and when to do it. There's a dictatorship that rules this country. So, how free are you? Well, you're not, they just say you are until you get out of line, then you'll see how free you are.

Let's say you come to America and you're not a citizen and they find out, they lock you up and deport you back to the country you came from. Now when they come, no one deports them when they find out they aren't a citizen of this country. Now, this is supposed to be a free country. Nothing here is really what it's supposed to be, other than you're in bondage. So see, man continues to suffer from being oppressed and it's always going to exist. So, don't be distracted by the ways of the world and don't be distressed from God's plan for you and always remember you're not of this world, you're just passing through.

By knowing that, you can learn to associate yourself around things that will uplift your spirit and always remember to appreciate the things you don't have less, known the things you do have like your health, loved ones, and life, and keep in mind that you are doing better than some and not worse than others.

Once again, there are many forms of bondages. Man enslave themselves by addiction and there are many types of addiction. Whatever man lets control his thoughts, feelings, and behavior is part of being in bondage. Whatever substance man chooses to do becomes his or her addiction. It starts out like this: at first, the substance uses the substance, then you use the substance, and then the substance uses you. Then you become powerless to that substance. At that point, you're a slave to whatever you're using and it takes control of you. Now the flipside is you can break that chain by not using or giving in to your addiction. Keep in mind that you are drink or hit from death. There is a power greater than man. You don't have to suffer all of your life, you can and will escape that bondage and be able to live without using and be able to deal with any circumstances you face.

You still voted for them. When you already knew the outcome, then you blame. The 45th president wasn't a politician at all, he was a corrupt businessman who only wanted to prove that he could be a better businessman for this country. It's all about checks and balances and trade goods. He wasn't all negative, he did some good for the American people, or should I say, for his kind, because nothing changed for the lower class people, they are still suffering as always. Politics is the biggest con game in the world. So see, society is like a big old sucker and the politicians keep licking because they're sweet. As they say, if you can trick them, you can beat them. It's sad but it's the truth and a lot of people don't like the truth, but it's better than a lie, wouldn't you say?

When it comes to the economy of this country, with all the consumption that's distributed, there's a great deal of trade with other countries all over. The American economy does not provide enough jobs for society. That is part of the reason why the crime rate is so high. They have a system that states if your actions don't qualify for this job or housing. And they talk about how great America is.

The American government does not care for the American people and that's part of America's problem. You have this group of people called the majority, which are the upper class people, and they're the ones that say what happens. People like the senator, governor, and other people in that bracket. Then you have the lower class people, which are the minority, and then you have what's called the disadvantaged minority, that society cast out because they either don't have an education or have a criminal history, things like that where society looks down on those people in a bad way.

They say the land of the proud and free. Really what's there to be proud of, with the lack of jobs and housing and the crime rate rising daily on top of that.

They enslave people like any other country.

There are so many reasons for bondage and here's a few: to have order among the people to get things done and so they can keep track of you and force people to do things that they want them to do. Without it, the world would be seriously out of control. No one would be safe, not like you're really safe now but there wouldn't be any civilizations among the people. Even with the law, it's still very dangerous. So in reality, being in bondage isn't a bad thing as it gives man some sort of structure.

Bondage is also for correction because when you become corrupt, they can take you and lock you up from society. At least that's what they do in America.

Now, when it comes to drug addiction, the government uses it as a form of control. So here's what they did, they made it affordable for society, that way they are able to use it on a select group of people to isolate them from society. In doing this, they are able to monitor their behavior and control them as slaves.

Now, those people that are using drugs become dependent on that substance and it's the cause of people losing their jobs, homes, and even breaking up families and the American society is alright with it, until it hits home. The government is okay with it as well.

Then it hit the president's home, so now there is a problem with drugs. Now they're concerned about the drug epidemic, now that it has spread across the country and into their homes. Now those addicted no longer go to prison, they get treatment. Because the drug made them commit the crime. Most addicts cannot work because they're habit won't allow them to. So they do whatever they have to do so they can support that habit.

It's all a part of control. Statistics show that in this country, drug addiction is a major part of bondage, which is part of population control.

It also keeps the American currency flowing, that's why the American dollar is used all over the world. You can not use any other country's currency in America.

It's like the game Monopoly, where you have control of a particular piece of property or business that gives you power. This is how they control the world.

These people, they get together and set a scale on what business or privilege they want the people to have or do. And then they put it into action. Now the slipside is it causes a great depression among society where they become dependent on the substance.

Which is one of the reasons for antidepressants. They say crime don't play but it does because when a person commits a crime to support the habit, they're another transformation of bondage, which is prison. A warehouse for slaves, they make big money off of each person in prison. The state along with other companies work those people for less than a slave's wage. It's a part of the monopoly game of the world, each prison has its own incorporation. It's bad enough they use your social security number; it's just like oil, they generate millions and you get nothing.

Now the drug trade plays a big part in today's economy, in today's society it's also a hot commodity; it's part of the stock market. It's the science that deals with the manufacturing, production, and distribution of the product. That consumes wealth and it relates to one of the various problems of society that deals with the economy. This is only to give some kind of confirmation about what is going on in the world. Let's not get things confused. I'm not saying that bondage is a bad thing, there is some good that comes from it.

Now back in the 1800s and 1900s, all these different ethenic groups came to America for a new life. They all had someone to represent them as a people. Those people stood for something and stood up for each other as well and supported each other. Each leader got together and formed what's called a union so that no one was left out. As time passed, that union became the local teamster union for the working class people of society. It's also part of the monopoly game. Which gives them control of the workforce. It's a good format that was set in place for everyone.

Well, today, society tries to hide racism but can't because of the superiority complex that exists in the world; it's not about color, it's about power.

I want to go back to the people in prison, some might say that's where they need to be. Okay, but they're not there for the crime. They are enslaved so that they can be forced to slave for pennies and top of that, you taxpayers are paying for their upkeep. Plus, they're making that state money for their slave wages. As I said earlier, there are different forms of bondages. Even though those people are being told what and when they can do things, they're not paying taxes.

Then there are some people whose situations are better than others, but, yes, the same as different classes of people. They're set up in groups. You have what's considered as the upper class, they have more freedom to do more than then the middle class people, who are a little better off than the low class people, who are trapped in an area where poverty is then you have below the under class people, the people society looks down on because they're homeless, drug addicts, and most of them were a part of the working class of society, being productive in society but the system wasn't there for them and so they gave up.

In our society, something went wrong. What happened to the togetherness that was once here, when people helped each other? It's like the more advanced we get, the further apart we become. What happened, does everyone feel that they don't need anyone or do they feel they're better than the next person? I don't know what it is. You need to know that no matter who you are, there's always going to be some form of bondage in this world we live in. And that ain't a bad thing. It's funny how time repeats itself, things that are happening now are things of the past. Many centuries ago they were killing for power, so, what are they doing today? The same. The same game, just different players.

There's so much hate in the world or greed that causes people to not have compassion for human life. Maybe it's the need to be in control or to feel like you're better than the next person. Fear is the only power that fears itself. Us as people don't really see the bondages we live in everyday and that's alright.

It's amazing that ever since this pandemic has been around, there've been a lot of racial events taking place on people of different ethnic groups. It's like the American white men feel like they're superior over the rest of the people and the law doesn't apply to them as a people. At what price will one pay for the things of this world, in exchange for his soul?

Because the son of man will be betrayed in the hands of men. From whom do the kings of the earth take taxes from? Their sons or from strangers? You know people do strange things for a small piece of change or power. What about you? Will you sell your soul for these worldly treasures or will you trust in the Lord to get you through?

Everyone has their own perspective about things that go on in life and I don't want anyone to be perplexed about or lose focus or get confused about the enslavement we suffer from. That everyone has a part in it and it's not all bad. Man is never free, it's all part of life in the world we live in. I'm sure we can empathize with one another when it comes to bondage.

BONDAGES

About the Author

Patrick A. Walton, author of Bondages book.

I was born in a little small city in Mississippi located at the top of the Delta named Charleston. I'm the second child of four born to Mrs. Janie Walton Shelton, my precious mother, whom I love dearly.

I was raised right but took a left turn. From there I went into bondages.

For most of my adult life I suffered from drug addiction. During that time in my life I was in bondages. There's different type of bondage that we suffer from. Through my pain and suffering and some choices I made in my addiction, it inspired me to share some views about bondages that's in this world we live in. Now, today I am sober and living a productive life.

Even though - we live in bondages, you don't have to stay in bondages and suffer. I thank God I got this opportunity to share some of my views about life and some of the things that's happening around the world. I would like to dedicate this book to my daughter, Chavon Henderson and my nephew, Desmond Walton. Whom I love with the utmost respect.

Thanks to my readers of Bondages,
Patrick Walton, Author

www.ingramcontent.com/pod-product-compliance
Lightning Source LLC
Chambersburg PA
CBHW071908070526
44583CB00016B/1892